Published by coProductions LLC, P.O. Box 236, Laurel, MD 20725.

    Editor and Designer: Colette Gingles

    Editorial Assistants: Diane Brown, Norma Hill and Samantha Reed

    Project Assistants: Morgan Gingles and Karen Smith

    Photographers: Terrence Nelson, Cipriana Thompson and Valerie Woody

    Make-up Artist: Tiffany Morand

TheWiseWomenProject.com

Printed in the United States of America. First Printing March 2011.

ISBN- 978-0-615-45534-1

in a different light

Reflections and Beauty of
Wise Women of Color
WISE WOMEN PROJECT: MARYLAND

Dorothy Bailey

FOREWORD BY JULIANNE MALVEAUX, PH.D.

Thank you!!
Dorothy bailey

preface

> "The best thing about aging is to be able to exhale."
> — Loretta Burgess, born 1939 —

IN A DIFFERENT LIGHT is not a work of fiction. Rather, it is a message to us all from 90 beautiful well-lived women who have stories to inspire us, to make us laugh, to make us think, to impart a special joy in our lives. *IN A DIFFERENT LIGHT* illuminates—not through the expansive rays of biographies or in-depth stories, but as a passing spotlight—a moment in the lives of women who have gathered wisdom for seven decades or more.

All of our "wisdom carriers" have lived 70 years or more. One celebrated her 100th birthday in May of 2010. Most are over 75 years of age with a dozen in their 90's. These women were here when air conditioning was invented and when frozen vegetables went on sale for the first time. Most were around when Ford introduced the Model B with a V-8 engine and when talking movies wowed theatergoers with their magic.

All of these marvelous women live in Maryland or have strong ties to the state. Some are married, and some are not. Some simply have no interest in the institution, and don't mind saying so! All of them have been, and continue to be, on life's journey. None of them is afraid to look back and assess her life. All of them have chosen to share the things that keep them going and the things they would have changed.

"If I knew then what I know now. ..." is a recurring theme. One says simply, "I'd do most things again, but I'd focus more on the journey, not the destination."

dedication

This book is dedicated

To my amazing parents Helen Gainey Thompson (1921-1976) and
Barto Thompson (1911-1972) who birthed me into a family where love reigned
supreme and developing the ability to think was a requirement

To my beloved siblings, Deanie (deceased), Kay, Xiney (deceased), Nikki and Anthony,
who never forgot, "You leave this house together and you'd better come back together"

To Robbin and Bart, my shining stars, my proudest accomplishments
and their wonderful spouses, Denny and Janine

To my remarkable grands, who brighten my life beyond my wildest expectations,
Mike, Kalil, Ivan, Little Denny (in heaven), and you too, Zy and little Nikki

To Grandpa Bailey, who I have thought about every day
since we met nearly fifty years ago..."You know"

To my nephews Cheeta and Darryl who left our family
and this world much better than they found it

To a host of sister angels whose earthly journeys did not last three-score-plus-ten,
especially; Evelyn Jenkins, Rachel Carter, Georgiana Scott, Linda Scott,
Vashti Smith Clark, Drusilla Jenkins and Helena Thompson

To the marvelous ladies whose photos and words grace these pages
and put meaning to the term wisdom carriers.

Dorothy Bailey

foreword

Dr. Julianne Malveaux

President, Bennett College for Women

the Senegalese proverb, "When an old person dies, a library burns to the ground," reminds us of the accumulated wisdom that each elder carries within her, and the obligation that each of us has to sit at her feet, learn her stories, and share her stories with those who come after us.

I am reminded of the Senegalese proverb when I flip through the rich pages of *In A Different Light: The Reflections and Beauty of Wise Women of Color* that was clearly lovingly compiled by Dorothy Bailey, a woman of accomplishment and a font of wisdom in her own right. In lifting up the stories of some of Maryland's wise women of color, Bailey not only preserves libraries that might otherwise burn, but also asserts the need for women of color to impart their wisdom, be it mother-wit, philosophical musing, or scholarly knowledge, just as others do.

Our culture disproportionately values the "wise words" of majority men, especially those whose lives have included some form of public service. Yet history belongs to she who holds the pen, and women's voices, especially the voices of women of color, are too often relegated to the periphery of public discourse. This is what makes *In A Different Light* such an amazing and important contribution.

There is a regal wisdom etched on the faces of so many of the women in this volume, a regality that reminds me of the late, great Dr. Dorothy Irene Height, a woman who playfully said that it took aging for her to appreciate being "fully clothed and in her right mind," something a minister once referenced when she was much younger. Until she was hospitalized in March 2010, just weeks before her transition on April 20, 2010, she went resplendently clothed to the office of the National Council of Negro Women, with, as always, her hat matching her shoes and the rest of her outfit. But as she was also fond of saying, the important thing was not what you wore ON your head, but what was IN your head. And at the office, Dr. Height was, as always, sharp with the kind of recall that many younger women found remarkably astounding. She could name the date, place and participants of meetings that took place decades ago. And, like the women in *In A Different Light*, she enjoyed mining her childhood and her young womanhood for lessons that could benefit younger women.

Not too long ago, I sat with Dr. Maya Angelou and Dr. Johnnetta Cole, giants, sheroes, and inspirations, and listened as they shared sister-wisdom about the aging process. Of course, there is the oft-repeated Bette Davis line, "Getting old isn't for sissies," or the line octogenarian Xernona Clayton often uses, "Age ain't nothing but a number, so I'll pick mine – 35." As these two beautiful, vital, servants seemingly bemoaned aging, there was sisterly companionship and simple joy in each other's company. And there were words of wisdom to be gleaned from a conversation that ranged from playful and joking to somber and serious.

It is fitting that Dorothy Bailey asked me to write this foreword at a time when I find myself in the "back nine" of life, having lived more years, at 57, than I am go' live. I spend more time than I'd care to admit marinating my own transition from brash bad girl to a seasoned sister who many see as a role model and elder. I can still manage, from time to time, to pop into a club, get my groove on, and even attract some under-40 attention. Yet when a younger brother told me that I shouldn't claim all my years and lie about my age, I asked him which years should I give back. If I claimed 45, which years would I erase? 1963, when as a 10-year-old, I watched the March on Washington on a scratchy black and white television? 1969, when the Free Huey Rally riveted San Francisco? 1974, the year of my college graduation? As Dr. Angelou says, "I wouldn't take nothing for my journey now." This book, this wisdom, reminds me to savor the space in which I find myself, and every moment, every millisecond, every experience that has led me to this space. As one of this book's wise women muses, "Sometimes I have to smile at myself; aging is not that bad."

Indeed, in our youth-oriented culture, it is worth remembering that aging is a blessing, that nothing is promised, and that in many cultures, especially African cultures, aging is revered, not disparaged, and wrinkles and gray hair are seen as beautiful evidence of a life well lived, not blemishes that should be addressed with a plastic surgery or other cosmetic aids. From the perspective of the Senegalese proverb, elders are seen as libraries, as repositories of knowledge and insight, as the sage foundation of our people's future.

In A Different Light is a splendid celebration of women, a celebration of wisdom and a celebration of life lessons and maturity. The women who share their musings are a reminder of the importance of oral histories, especially those of women of color, which are often uncollected. And they are inspiration! I want to do 70-plus with the same dignity, splendor, and wisdom as these women! Thank you, Dorothy Bailey, for this wonderful gift.

"For I know the plans I have for you," says the Lord. "They are plans for good and not for disaster, to give you a future and a hope. In those days when you pray, I will listen.
– Jeremiah 29:11-12 NLT –

acknowledgements

THANK YOU GOD FOR LISTENING AND FOR ANSWERED PRAYERS.

This project could not have been completed without the
help, gentle and not so gentle encouragements and directions from some
amazing people who showed up as blessings and answered prayers.

The first blessing: Ciprana Thompson, the primary photographer, who knew
that I did not know what I was talking about, but was willing to get on board anyway.
She brought with her Terrance Nelson, whose kind sprit and keen eye for photography
calmed us all. She also added make-up artist Tiffany Moran with her little bag of magic.

Colette Gingles, who used her creative genius, her brilliance and her patience to
make this project come alive. Thank you Colette for pushing, prodding, pleading, providing
above and beyond, a blessing to this project and to me. Karen Smith, just showed up one day
and started filling gaps that I did not know were there. She brought such Godly energy
to the project. Valerie Woody, the incredible other photographer.

More blessings: Dorothy Boddie, Robbin Brittingham, Diane Brown, Patrice Ficklin, Annette Funn,
Donna Crocker Mason, Juanita Miller, Ramona Purnell, Howard Stone, Alethia Strake, Debyi Thomas,
Willie Wood and Jacqueline Woody. Each of you sent some beautiful, incredible ladies my way.

Oretha Bridgwaters, Elsie Conway, Mary Godfrey, Rowena Morgan, your homes became our
studios and I am grateful for your hospitality and generosity. Elaine Barton, Lionel Bailey,
Kay Butler, Hildagrade Connor, Tressie Griffin, Bonnie Jones, Carita Miles, Mae Pica,
Anthony Thompson, Nikki Thompson and Glenda Wilson, please hear me say,
"Thank you for listening, listening, and then, listening again!"

Thank you Chaplain Black. I used your suggestion.

I am grateful to the many friends—you know who you are—
who always asked, always encouraged and always had a prayer ready.

Wisdom is better than weapons of war

Ecclesiastes 9:18

I grew up in a small North Carolina community where the labels "senior citizen" or "old" were never used.

Our elders were simply referred to as Mister or Miss—Mr. Malcolm, Miss Eunice, Miss Janie. They were the wise and they were the respected—the authorities responsible for helping to raise us all.

They were the advisers, counselors, teachers, bearing lessons from the school of hard knocks. They prayed for you and, from time to time, had "a little piece of change" to spare. Their doors were always unlocked, and your voice calling their name as you entered was their door bell. While most of the elders in my community were uneducated or under-educated, they were family. Only when I was an adult did I realize that many could not read. These individuals—these wonderful individuals—are my youthful remembrance of what it was to be, dare I say, old.

My mother was 19 when I was born. She died before she was 60, and in my mind she will forever be young and beautiful.

As I reflected on age for this project I realized it was difficult for me to remember women in their seventies and eighties when I was growing up. Those Misters and Misses I grew up with were mostly in their late fifties or early sixties. During the late 1940s and 1950s, the life expectancy of many African American women was around 56 years. I'd never had a real reason to explore the questions of aging and life, of what it is to be a woman, a black woman past the age of 50, until a fateful spring day.

One beautiful April afternoon my 4-year-old grandson Ivan and I were traveling down Highway 501 near Lancaster, Pennsylvania. It was a peaceful ride, not much traffic, and you could see green grass and trees for what seemed like forever. Momentarily, Ivan spoke, leaning forward against the restraint of his car seat. "Grandma," he said, "are you 100 years old?"

"No, Ivan," I replied amused.

Curious, he questioned again. "Are you 50?"

"No, Ivan," I answered, "much older."

Satisfied, Ivan sat back content to stare at passing trees and grass, but I was intrigued by his question about age. Is there really a difference between being 100 and 50? Does it look the same to Ivan? To me? Was I different from those Misters and Misses I remembered from when I was a child? Was I different than I was 10 years ago, five years, even two years ago? Should I be?

After delivering Ivan safely to his parents I sat down with pen and paper determined to think this thing through. I was born in 1940 so...I was almost...70 years old! Almost three score plus ten, the phrase penned in the 90th Psalm:

> *"The days of our years are threescore and ten, and if by reason of strength they be fourscore years."*

I was familiar with the words. As an elected official I'd hosted an event honoring senior women entitled Three Score Plus Ten. It had been a joyous celebration saluting beautiful women who'd contributed to the community. It was humbling to think that soon, and very soon, I would be one of those women. A woman who'd lived for 70 years.

GATHERING WISDOM

Seventy years. They have been eventful years, to say the least. Years filled with everything that comes to make and form a life. Things you learn and things you learn to change.

I can go back to days on my Aunt Esther's porch. Her porch was a meeting place. She had a steel bench in her front yard and on that bench, on that porch, all problems, all issues were discussed and handled. That yard was the place where reputations could be enhanced or destroyed, marriages were fixed, mended or done away with, preachers were praised or just plain talked about. As a child, that bench, that porch, was also a point of praise, embarrassment, encouragement or even a spanking. But I was always good; I never wanted to say or do anything that would cause my parents to be ashamed of me. I studied hard, had good manners and did the right thing. I was Helen and Barto's smart daughter.

I remember being told very early on not to wear red, as it was an inappropriate color for decent women, and most especially dark-skinned women. I accepted that as gospel, very seldom wearing the color as a child, though it was one that I loved.

Then one summer when I was about 14, I served as a delegate to a Sunday School convention. The convention included an all-girls workshop during which we discussed a number of things—dressing appropriately, good manners, proper behavior, and the like. Sitting mostly as a spectator during the conversations I finally raised a nervous hand to ask the discussion leader if she thought dark girls could wear red. I will never forget her broad smile as she pointed to the red ribbon pinned to my blouse. She said, "Take the ribbon from your blouse and place it next to your face."

As I did, her smile grew even wider. She told me that I looked great, that I could most certainly wear red.

just pure joy

In late eighties, I was a guest at a very formal dinner with, oh, about a thousand other people. Much to my delight, my son and some of his college friends traveled to attend the same event. Later my son told me that when they entered the crowded dinner hall one of his classmates said, "You will never find your mom with all these people." My son, said he responded, "Man, you don't know my mom. She stands out in a crowd!"

On my most trying difficult days, I can hear my son's non-expressive voice telling me this story and it always makes me smile. Pure joy, not because it is true but because my son said so.

BORN September 6, 1940

dorothy bailey

She said I could wear any color I ever thought to wear. It was then I learned that as an individual, I could make my own decisions. I could make decisions that were best for me. To this very day I wear lots and lots of red.

I've learned other lessons in my life, some not so easily fixed by removing a ribbon from your blouse. I learned that marriage was not what I had dreamed or hoped it would be. That it can be difficult, that it was difficult. Through my marriage I was taught lessons of betrayal, infidelity and unfaithfulness. It was not at all what I'd expected or wanted. But what came through the moving tides of shock and devastation was the tenacity to hold fast to God's unchanging hand.

I also learned the value of true friendships. Being married I often felt devastatingly broken, but my friends would not let me fall. They rallied as a true fence around me providing love and support that helped me grow until I realized I was stronger than I ever imagined I could be. I learned the importance of moving forward. They encouraged me to hold my head up, put one foot in front of the other, not to look back and to stay focused on my goals. I learned that if I looked up I would see the Cross, and that had meaning in my life and gave meaning to my life. That cross helped me to stay focused and fight the good fight of faith. So it was then, and so it remains now.

THE WISDOM CARRIERS

Seventy years. There is so much to remember about my life. But that spring day after being questioned by my grandson I found myself also reflecting on the lives of the many incredible women I've met over the years. I wondered what they were doing, who they had become, if they kept joy in their lives, what had they seen, experienced, who and how had they loved. How would they be remembered?

Moreover, how would I be remembered? What brings me joy? How did I want to spend the rest of my life? There were more and more questions I grew increasingly determined to answer, so I decided to go in search of myself through the lives of phenomenal women, wise women, women born before 1940.

This Wise Women Project has brought me more joy and gratitude than I could have ever imagined. These women, these *Wisdom Carriers*, are so different in so many ways—profession, education, income, marital status—yet so similar in others, so caring and compassionate, fiercely independent, self-assured with uncompromised senses of humor and unshakable confidence. Yet not one of them was arrogant, proud yes, but also grateful and humble, courageous and clearly thankful for each and every blessing.

I visited and talked to well over a hundred women who live across the state of Maryland or who have strong ties to the state. Some are public and popular figures, yet most are women whose name you may never see printed in a newspaper, up in lights, or posted on a website. They are women whose lives have been rich, full, and oh so wonderful. Women, who did what some would call the ordinary things, like instill dreams, pride and the desire to succeed in their children. Women who proudly say my child has her doctorate or other degree from a school that at one time they were not allowed to attend because of their race.

There are women who talk about their grandchildren as if they could fly. Women who almost brought tears to my eyes as they described the love they shared with their husbands. But also women who knew that their marriages were not what they had dreamed for themselves and who had to make other choices, had to do what they had to do to save themselves and save their children.

Women who grew up when we were not "of color," but "colored." One woman could hardly talk about what she endured being dark skinned and having her hair straightened with a hot comb while the hair grease popped and burned her neck and face. She remembers going to parties better dressed than her friends but not being asked to dance because of her complexion. Another remembers Ocean City being a segregated community where blacks were allowed on the beach and boardwalk only on certain days. She says she still trembles when she thinks about it. And yet another recalls allowing the corner store merchant to believe she was white when she went there to buy snacks and supplies for her graduate school classmates. She later realized the potential danger.

Women who worked alone from "can't see in the morning to can't see at night." Women who sacrificed for their mates and their children. Women who believed in service to others, giving back because of the blessings they received. Women who raised and helped out with other people's children. One opened her home to a nephew who had been jailed. When she talked about him you could see her hope and prayer for his success.

Many of the women talked about the compassion, passion and honesty in their relationships—how they adored their mates, their children and their friends. They discussed their travels and exposing their children to places and experiences that at one time they could only dream about. And there were some who talked about turning pain into joy. How it felt to have to raise children alone—how hard it was not to have your husband—your children's father provide for them or be involved in their lives.

They shared very personal stories with me. Some vocalized thoughts they had never spoken before: I should have had more children, I should not have had as many children, I should not have had any children. So, for this project, I extracted tidbits of advice, snippets from a lesson learned, or a snapshot of a favorite memory that they were comfortable sharing with everyone.

It quickly became evident that their words should be paired with photographs. That in documenting their reflections on life we should document them as well, a lasting tribute to the beauty of each. To the immutable spirit that led one woman to arrive at the photo session in her Mercedes convertible sharing how she loves to drive with the top down, or another to say she had limited time to share with us, and then with a wink walked away with a smiling fellow on her arm. And, I will never forget the lady who cried when I asked her to sit with a photographer for a photo session. When I explained to her we were trying to capture beautiful women she said, "No one has ever told me that I was beautiful."

Those photo sessions, scheduled to be efficient and businesslike, quickly turned into a house party, women laughing and sharing, catching up and

swapping stories finding similarities in their singular experiences. From them emerged some of the most fulfilling moments of this project, some of the most amazing, laugh-inducing, quotes:

> ... I still laugh every time I think about my mother's "little talk" with me. She said, "Always remember to keep your panties up and your dress down." For a moment I had trouble figuring out how I was going to go to the bathroom. ...

> ... It is always interesting to hear people say "I am going to be just like you when I get your age." I often wonder, how? ...

Others speaking towards life's important lessons:

> ... I have lived long enough to really learn how to forgive. It was not easy but I did. Some folk in my husband's family thought I was too dark and did not have enough education to marry into their family. Life is interesting, many of those same ones, later in life, I had to help. I had to bury. I had to learn to forgive.

And still others revealing the simplest truth:

> ... sometimes I have to smile at myself ... aging is not that bad.

In the end this project, Wise Women, is about celebrating and honoring the wisdom, beauty, strength and courage of the three score plus ten and more women. It is the opportunity to see and listen to these women, and it is a testament that a life 70 years after birth is one filled with good works, good service. One filled with love and one that is still very much worth living.

in a different light

the wisdom carriers

IN A DIFFERENT LIGHT

Eva Anderson   Pocahontas Y. Ashe   Barbara B. Atkinson   Frances Owens Austin   Ertie F. Barnes   Erma Barron   Joanne Benson   Willia Bland   Elizabeth Bouey-Yates   Lila Brighthaupt

WISE WOMEN OF COLOR

Naomi Elliott   Amanda E. Feggans   Mattie Giles   Mary H. Godfrey   Doris Rice Goodlett   Margaret Gray   Mildred Ridgley Gray   Lillian Green   Rebecca F. Griffin   Dora S. Halton

RELECTIONS & BEAUTY

Helen M. Hutchinson   Shirley A. Jackson   Charline Lewis Jacob   Alverta Franklin Johnson   Bernice Lee Johnson   Sarah J. Johnson   Ada M. Jones   Christine M. Jones   Flossie C. Keck   Beatrice V. Leonard

MARYLAND

Juanita E. Orr   Winnie S. Parker   Hilda R. Pemberton   Virgie B. Phifer   Ollie Miller Phillips   Edna Poney   Doris Porter   Elizabeth G. Proctor   Catherine Robinson   Rita L. Robinson

WISDOM CARRIERS

Thelma Harris Taylor   Beatrice P. Tignor   Jacqueline C. Tolson   Joyce Moore Turner   June Turner   Lucy B. Warr   Ezola M. Webb   Mary A. West   Bertha Wilson   Rita Scott Womack

MARYLAND

Mary Budd   Loretta A. Burgess   Louie Dell Clark   Elsie R. Conway   Marie Cooper   Annie Crocker   Juliette H. Curry   Vivian Dodson   Lauranita T. Dugas   Jacqueline A. Eley

WISDOM CARRIERS

Barbara Harris   Elizabeth K. Henderson   Norma L. Hill   Anna M. Hodges   Ertha Lee Hopkins   Catherine D. Horn   Sarah Gladys Horne   Carolyn J. B. Howard   Gwendolyn M. Howard   Evelyn H. Husbands

WISE WOMEN OF COLOR

Ruth Leonard   Helen Sylvester Lewis   Virginia M. Manning   Barbara F. Martin   Jean Ann Gray Matthews   Peola H. McCaskill   Rose W. Miller   Rowene D. Morgan   Elaine M. Neal   Frances M. Newman

IN A DIFFERENT LIGHT

Cynthia C. Rollins   Fleeta R. Ruffin   Alberta Louise Seymour   Mollie Sherrod   Doris J. C. Spencer   Muriel Springets   Mamie Stanley   Daisy H. Stith   Constance D. Sturgis   Essie Sutton

Gratitude would certainly be my theme—first, to my missionary parents who instilled in me at a very early age the desire to serve, to share blessings, to help others and above all, to believe and keep the faith!

My gratitude also extends to the many people I have met and who have walked with me. I am grateful for the love given and received and for the rich experiences of this life's journey!

BORN *June 11, 1925*

elizabeth bouey-yates

Knowledge is learned—and life has taught me much

Things I felt so passionately about in my young life matter so little now. Looking back, I smile at how serious I thought everything was. Promotions, new cars, a bigger house, a thinner body, being well liked, being recognized, having stylish clothes, having smart mannerly children and having an attentive husband. These were important then.

Now my list of passions include faith, love, friendship and caring for others. As we age the list of passions grows shorter. What remains on the list, however, has been tested by the heat of life's journey and endures like pure gold.

BORN *October 21, 1937*

mary godfrey

Patience was Mom's strong suit—six single births in ten years—five daughters to shape into proper little ladies. She handled this task with such finesse that each child believed, "I'm her favorite!"

Joy readily fills my heart as I recall my desire as a young girl to wear a "suit blouse," just like my mom. I wanted so very much to be like her and tried fashioning myself after her. Even today, I still follow many of her instructions, such as, "Coordinate your clothing, wear clothes that compliment your body, and try not to wear more than three different colors with one outfit."

My siblings often say to me, "You remind me of Mom." And I say out loud, "Really?" In my heart, I'm screaming, "YES!"

BORN January 29, 1940

elizabeth

kelly henderson

If I knew then what I know now,
I'd do the same thing.
Just because!

BORN *June 21, 1926*

dora halton

I have reached the age of 73, a woman in good health sharing my home with my 94-year-old healthy mother. Having close relationships with family and friends over the years, including some from elementary school, high school and college that I continue to communicate with, has added many happy and healthy moments to my life.

Wasting no time thinking over what some may consider regrets, I am happy to report that I am content with life and pray that I will continue to let God be my guide. I am not sure what I knew THEN, but NOW I know that God has blessed me.

BORN *May 19, 1937*

charline jacob

If I knew then what I know now, I would have done it the same way—running this race with patience and trusting God to do the rest.

BORN *December 31, 1915*

helen sylvester lewis

After all is said and done, if I knew then what I know now, there isn't much that I would change. I would hope to eliminate any pain that I might have inflicted upon others and certainly opt to erase some that I experienced. Nevertheless, my experiences have made me who I am and the journey has not been dull.

One change might have robbed me of some of the most rewarding experiences of my life. Besides, who knows if any change would have produced a better result? God has been good to me during these oh so many years and I certainly believe the best is yet to come.

BORN *January 8, 1931*

juliette
curry

If I had known in my youth what I know now, I wouldn't want to change anything because everything happens according to God's plan. I know that God loves me and that his grace and mercy will sustain me.

BORN *May 11, 1928*

jacqueline eley

I do believe that the greatest gift that anyone can give is the gift of love. Love is not the diamond ring or the fur coat or the trip to Hawaii. Love is the boy from the neighborhood coming over to help chop your row of cotton in the blazing hot sun. Love is your dad raising pigs to take to the market to pay your college tuition. Love is your mother cooking your favorite pot of soup to welcome you home from school.

Love is your husband driving to you during a snowstorm so you can follow his car tracks home. Love is that little thing you cannot touch; you just know in your heart that it is there.

BORN *July 25, 1940*

The best thing about aging is to be able to exhale. You're still on the journey but the ride is smoother and the scenery is more beautiful—this season is truly the best part of the journey.

As I continue my life's journey, I strive to make a positive difference in the lives of others along the way. I am available to listen, offer advice when requested, provide support when possible and say "I love you" often...and really mean it.

I survived challenges because I believe in a power greater than myself and I have truly learned to enjoy life.

BORN *July 30, 1939*

loretta **burgess**

I remember two story books that were given to me by my father when I was in first grade. One was *Little Black Sambo* which held no insult for me—I just loved the story and pictures. The other book, *Sammy Goes Around the World*, inspired me to want to learn about other people and places.

When I was seven, my aunt gave me a cooking range and a little black doll that I named Rachel after my cousin. I still have the range and the doll.

Thank God that at that tender young age I was not aware of racism and prejudice. That was to come later.

BORN *April 26, 1925*

constance
sturgis

I meet my husband at Drake University. He was in law school while I was an undergraduate student. The day we met, he was coming out of the law school building and stopped to chat with me. He asked me to attend a legal society ball. Of course, I said, "Yes!"

Later, in 1957, shortly after the birth of our son, we moved to Baltimore from Des Moines, Iowa. Baltimore was so different from Des Moines. I had never been around so many black people before and it was indeed exciting. There was an energy to the city—a style, a rhythm, an intellect and passion—that made the people of Baltimore amazing.

My husband and I became involved in all aspects of Baltimore life including social, civil rights and political. We marched against segregated housing and protested a host of other injustices. We invested in and became part of our new hometown.

BORN *October 1, 1927*

gwen howard

I am grateful for the encouragement of my grandmother to be the best, to do the best and to trust in the Lord.

BORN *April 7, 1937*

lillian green

I got married at the age of 20, and once I started my family, gave up my plans of going to nursing school. Now, I have four grandchildren and one great-grandchild. The irony is that one of my grandchildren is a successful registered nurse who looks after me. I now understand that my earlier sacrifices turned out to be a larger blessing in the end. I wouldn't change a thing.

BORN *January 16, 1925*

bernice johnson

I'd do most things again, but I'd focus more on the journey, not the destination.

An older wiser woman than I often said that if you knew what was "round that corner" you probably wouldn't go. She was right, of course.

I am grateful that I learned early on that life is full of uncertainties and that one should be prepared to adjust to changes and shifts in circumstances. Do I believe that one has no control over one's life and is therefore not responsible for what happens? No. I believe that I have an awesome responsibility to be prepared to seize the opportunities afforded me and to deal with the barriers and blocks that may lie just around the corner.

I am grateful for the roots and wings that are my heritage. Roots that anchor me to the past, and secure me in the present, and wings that have always allowed me to soar toward a promising, though never taken for granted, future. Through it all, I have been empowered to rise above those barriers that are sometimes just around the corner.

If I knew then what I know now ... I'd have paid more attention to "the rules." ... I'd have paid less attention to "the rules." ... I'd have been more tolerant of those for whom change and uncertainty seemed more difficult. ... I'd have realized just how smart my Dad was, and asked him more questions. ... I'd have known how challenging it must have been to be my mother. ... I'd have appreciated just how fortunate I am, and let those who made it possible know it. ... I'd have still married E. Gordon Goodlett forty years ago. ... I'd have learned to swim a lot earlier in life.

BORN June 15, 1939

doris
goodlett

beatrice tignor

IF I KNEW THEN what I know now, I would have given more time to cultivating sincere relationships. I would have spent more quality time building a stronger family. I would have created a greater sense of moral responsibility and given more time and service to those less fortunate than I. I would have learned more about the world and traveled to all of its corners to seek truths in philosophical and religious differences. While climbing the career ladder, I would have listened more to those wiser and more experienced to become more flexible in my thinking. Yet, I would still believe that women can make it alone. While I revere the institution of marriage, I don't believe it is for everyone. And women should not feel guilty for not being married, but proud of finding a positive way to build a life for themselves.

BORN June 2, 1939

My mother was the launching pad for my success. From her I learned to see the light without being blinded by it. From my mother I learned to be humble and compassionate, set goals, stay focused, dream and have vision.

Today's vision is tomorrow's reality.

BORN *December 25, 1929*

christine jones

Even if I knew then what I know now, there are no affective changes that I would make in my life, for I am grateful to my God, my family, mentors and friends for the blessed life that I have lived for 77 years.

The course of my life was determined by my parents to whom I am eternally grateful. During the days of segregation, they foresaw a better life for their children if we were college educated. And what a wonderful life it has been enriching the academic lives of my students as a teacher in Florida, New York, France, Germany and California; broadening my understanding of and empathy for many people while traveling the world with family and, most of all, giving back, through the years, politically, financially and as a volunteer at many levels.

BORN *April 19, 1933*

*juanita*orr

My life has always been about God, family and an awareness of the needs and desires of others. Many past times are enjoyable to me but none so much as watching things grow. **Watching the beauty of a flower** in bloom keeps me always aware of the miracles of God. As one writer puts it, "Happiness is a wayside flower that grows along the highway of usefulness."

BORN November 3, 1932

If I knew then what I know now, I would have...

- **...** spent more time in prayer.

- **...** entered the ministry of Jesus Christ at an early age.

- **...** lived a more Christ-centered and God-focused life.

- **...** gone to school to become a domestic violence counselor.

- **...** worked harder at pleasing God and not have been such a people pleaser.

- **...** honored myself as one of God's special angels and I would not have accepted people abusing me.

- **...** spent more time with my family playing, singing, dancing laughing, traveling and having fun.

BORN *September 5th*

virginia manning

My gratitude is to my grandfather, Lewis Ridgeley, an ex-slave and minister, for his firm belief in God. He firmly believed that home, church and school could make a difference in the lives of mankind.

BORN *September 24, 1920*

mildred gray

Continue to get the most of life daily, for tomorrow is not promised

I can remember my grandfather telling me about the day the slaves were freed. He recalled that he had lost a cap given to him by the slave owner. He was out looking for this cap because if he went back without it, he would surely get a beating from the slave master.

While he was out, he heard a woman calling his name. When he saw this woman, who had been sold to another slave-owner, he told her why he was out looking for his cap. She shouted to him, "Don't worry about that cap. We's free! We's free!"

Overjoyed he ran into the arms of the woman. That woman was his mother.

BORN *February 4, 1915*

lila **brighthaupt**

God blessed in my lifetime...
  ... a happy childhood—loving family
  ... a pleasant youth—progressive growth
  ... a professional adulthood—caring friends
  ... and now the senior years—enjoying the days with
  minimal trials and with assurance of God's love.

BORN *December 30, 1925*

elsie conway

I was inspired by the death of Dr. Martin Luther King in 1968, to establish a modeling studio to support women and young girls through training in personal awareness and self-esteem. I believe that we all have a responsibility to volunteer and affect the quality of life in the community. I believe part of my assignment is to find beauty and highlight it. So after forty-plus years managing an institution and holding fast to my assignment, when many are feeling the urge to slow down, on most days, I feel like I am just beginning to kick into high gear.

BORN May 28, 1925

willia bland

virgie phifer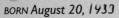

BORN *August 20, 1933*

barbara martin

BORN *August 30, 1922*

amanda teggans

BORN *February 21, 1925*

I am so grateful for the longevity of my marriage to a loving and caring husband. My fiftieth wedding anniversary celebration is something I will always remember.

Once I got married I had to always remember I was no longer single and had to consider two people in my thoughts and actions. We had ups and downs but both worked at keeping our marriage together and making decisions together. He died a decade ago and I still miss him a lot.

I remember hearing a story of true love... "The 25-year-old school teacher rode five miles every day to teach in a one-room school. After a year of making fires at the school and babysitting her horse and buggy, the 50-year-old bachelor married her." ...the story of my parents.

I have been married most of my life.
I know for sure, marriage should not be
taken lightly. When you get married you
make a commitment to each other. And
you only get out of marriage what you are
willing to put into it. If you put God first
in your marriage, then eventually
everything will work out.

BORN *November 3, 1931*

flossie
keck

> # "The world is a book, and those who do not travel read only a page."
>
> — *St. Augustine* —

I have traveled often, whenever and wherever I decided I wanted to go. Yet my trip to Peru and Ecuador was more than a vacation; it was truly an expedition—a once in a lifetime experience. While there I traveled by train, bus and dingy. I climbed mountains and more mountains. In Ecuador, I stood with both feet on both sides of the equator.

All in all I am so grateful to have had these experiences. God allowed me to go to the mountaintops and see His glory and infallibility on display.

I am convinced, however, that these trips should be done before the 50-year mark. I never want to climb another mountain and look forward to my next luxury cruise. Yes, that is my kind of lifestyle at this point in my life!

BORN *June 4, 1940*

shirley jackson

I have spent my entire life as a teacher, community leader and public servant, working to make a difference. You see, my parents didn't stand for "no foolishness," and neither do I.

BORN *March 11, 1941*

joanne benson

I am the oldest of 13 and am most grateful for my family. I cherish the memories of growing up where there was always discipline and love from my parents, grandparents, aunts and uncles as well as members of my hometown and church family.

After all these years, the greatest gift that I can remember given to me was in 2009 when my four children honored me with a 75th birthday celebration.

BORN *December 19, 1934*

jean matthews

I especially remember my youth, growing up in the Virgin Islands ... sun, sand, sea, church and enjoying large family gatherings.

BORN *February 1, 1937*

ada jones

I am sincerely grateful to my elementary school teachers who helped me develop a love for learning that I have maintained throughout my adult life.

As simple as it sounds, I still remember their grooming advice: "Keep your long hair from making the collar of your clothes dirty."

BORN *October 18, 1931*

rose miller

Life in a small town was very simple.

Women worked at home and most people had a house with a garden. Practically everyone walked; cars were few. There were buses to major cities and streetcars in our county. A favorite journey was a 25 mile streetcar ride on a Sunday afternoon.

My life revolved around home, church, school, Girl Scout Troop, reading, and the radio. My classmates, mostly children of coal miners, spent long hours on county buses to get an education. Their southern migrant parents made big sacrifices for them to live a better life.

Segregation existed in employment, education, restaurants and theaters and there were few black (colored) professionals. Once you graduated high school, you faced the challenge of finding and qualifying for a job. This meant leaving home and hoping for luck.

I am grateful for parents who realized the value of education and searched for family involvement for advancement.

BORN *May 9, 1920*

rowene morgan

I thank God for the skin I am in! It is good to know that you don't need to copy or try to make yourself look or be like anyone else. God created you and you are His original. No one else can be you. You are a designer original.

BORN *January 17, 1938*

pocahontas ashe

I am grateful for my parents and grandparents who taught me rules that have served me well through the years, especially the act of forgiveness. Forgiveness is one of the greatest acts that one can perform. It frees the mind of negativity, therefore allowing the creation of new positive thoughts.

BORN *December 18, 1925*

helen hutchinson

It has been said that seeing is believing. I believe you must use the "correct eye" to make that possible.

BORN *March 10, 1936*

doris porter

My life has been rich with many memories. A visit to the
Island of Goree in Senegal, West Africa, was truly a profound and life changing gift. As I witnessed the "door of no return," the place from which many of our forefathers were shipped into slavery, I experienced almost every emotion humanly possible. I felt anger, sadness, disappointment, joy, happiness, and thankfulness. All these emotions reflect on how we as African Americans have survived and prospered despite how or where we began. It reaffirmed my belief that I can do all things through Christ who strengthens me.

In 1992 I had the great opportunity to travel to Israel. While there I visited many religious sites that were precious to me; however the one that has left a lasting impression was my visit to the Holocaust Museum. While there it was not so much the items of the museum, but the teachers, telling their very young students about the Holocaust. They were telling them of the horrors of the Holocaust so that those events would never be repeated. As I watched, I felt very guilty that our history of slavery and civil rights struggles has not been shared with most of our children. Our children need to know that they have survival skills and that they do not have to repeat the struggles of our past.

Another gift of remembrance was the opportunity to participate in the historic inauguration of the Black Caucus for the Parliament of England in April 1989. My participation renewed my commitment to being a more focused elected official.

IF I KNEW THEN . . .

If I knew then how much joy and satisfaction could be gained in serving God, I would have been more committed sooner. As a person who likes to fix things and make things right, I have learned that if you trust God, He will work it out for you better and faster than you can.

If I knew then what I know now I may have worked a little longer (not necessarily harder) to save my marriage for the sake of my children. I realize now the impact our separation had on the long-term mental health of my children. However, the need for a father figure cannot be replaced either in or out of the marriage.

BORN June 29, 1940

hilda pemberton

I am grateful that in my life there were so many who stretched my skills and abilities and encouraged my efforts, so failure was not an option. These humble people taught lessons that paved the road for the fulfillment of my aspirations and the successes and abundance I have today. My greatest desire is to pass on their practices, attitudes and value system.

BORN *October 25, 1932*

I realized very early that I had to work hard to achieve my goals. I am blessed because I had the support of parents, siblings and folk in my community. Our parents pushed all of us to always do our best. Neither of my parents graduated from high school. Our parents would say, "I didn't have the opportunity to go to high school and beyond, but all 11 of our children will." And we all did!

BORN May 19, 1935

ezola webb

My parents loved us dearly but they were strict. One of my father's favorite sayings was, "Water seeks its level." That was his constant reminder to us that you are judged by the company you keep.

BORN September 6, 1917

bertha wilson

If I knew then what I know now, I would have continued my education to become a doctor. When I graduated from college, schools in Georgia were segregated and there were no 'colored' medical schools in the state.

At that time, I did not know there was a federal law stating that since Georgia had refused to educate me in-state, they would have to pay my out-of-state tuition to any school in the nation accepting me. What I know now is that information—or the lack of information—made a difference in the life paths I took.

BORN June 2, 1932

thelma taylor

I am grateful for my upbringing in the church. We had a minister and his wife who loved children and did much to influence young people. I still have some reading materials they gave to me 60 years ago. Their influence was so great that I wish I had done more in the line of Christian ministry. At this point, I stay involved with Bible study groups and Christian music. The decision to move to a senior community has afforded me the time and opportunity to follow this passion.

BORN *September 17, 1928*

rebecca griffin

Growing up we didn't have all the things we wanted but God provided all we needed. My mother, who lived to be 109, started us off in the church in 1949 and I am still there. I have been a musician in my church for over 60 years. I am a colon cancer survivor and as I look back, I know it was God who gave me strength and intestinal fortitude. Going through those experiences, I was inspired to write songs to the glory of God.

born March 24, 1935

winnie parker

If I knew then what I know now, my service to others would have been greatly enhanced. Earlier knowledge would have allowed me to reflect on simple joys and be even more effective in public service.

BORN December 20, 1938

carolyn howard

Effective communication is the greatest thing of all. It matters not whether it is with your husband, children, friends, coworkers, relatives or neighbors. When you talk things out, you may find your story to be completely different from the way someone else may have perceived it to be. Whatever the situation, talk it out.

BORN February 14, 1924

essie sutton

If I knew then what I know now my life would be different because I would have gone into the ministry. I thank God for letting me live this long and to witness so many, many changes. Things are different now: kerosene lamps, now electricity; outhouses, now indoor bathrooms; $6.25 weekly wages was considered good money, now some people make more money than they know what to do with.

BORN November 16, 1922

mamie stanley

The love and values instilled in me by my parents were remarkable gifts. I was the only African American in my class from first grade to graduation. My mother's struggles helped me, my children and grandchildren.

There is not a lot I would change in my life. Perhaps I may have put some things on hold— married a little later. My advice would be to make sure you marry someone who is a good friend, someone who respects you as well as loves you. Respect one another and pray a lot.

BORN *March 24, 1929*

barbara brooks atkinson

I don't sit home and feel sorry for myself. I have had a good life. I was married to my husband for 64 years, we had 9 wonderful children. I now have 15 grandchildren, 27 great-grandchildren and 3 great-great-grands. After our children were grown, we spent many years traveling together. I live alone now and am still very active. I go to church, I belong to a senior citizen club and yes, I play BINGO. I will even cook for myself when I feel like it.

BORN *April 15, 1920*

ruth leonard

I was married to my husband for 62 years and I miss him so. I had a wonderful husband—he was a good father. We both lost our mothers very early, long before we went to high school, and we had to "kind of" take care of ourselves. Maybe that was one of the reasons we worked so hard to have a good relationship, support one another and be good parents. We took our children on a vacation and then we would always take one by ourselves. Sometimes children just need a break from parents ... and parents need a break from their children.

BORN *March 7, 1928*

alverta johnson

My advice to those getting married is be loving, be upfront, work together have special time for each other—I believe it is called date night now. When choosing a mate look for your values in the other person. It is important to like your spouse as well as love that person.

BORN *February 20, 1926*

muriel springett

Gratitude ... for life, for love, for family, for friends

For my dad ... who gave me a sense of joy
the ability to appreciate life and
to see the humor in most situations

For my mom ... who taught me to appreciate the finer things
in life like books, art, music and travel, and instilled in me
the confidence to be all that I could be

For my three brothers and three sisters ... who taught me
valuable lessons, helped me to understand that we all see
the world through different lenses and that is okay

For my husband ... who gave me love,
total acceptance, over 50 years of marriage,
four beautiful children

For my four children ... who took me down many
interesting paths, led me in unexpected adventures, made
my life complete, filled me with joy (most of the time)

For my four grandchildren ... who gave me an opportunity
to love unconditionally, opened my eyes to the wonders of
the universe, taught me the real meaning of love

For my friends ... who accept me as I am and
who make the circle complete

BORN October 11, 1936

rita robinson

I am most grateful to have been given the opportunity to be in public service. That role allowed me to have a ride on Air Force One and talk face to face with President Clinton. I am grateful that my mother lived long enough to see my success.

vivian dodson

I once heard someone say, "When I look back, I am grateful, and when I look forward I am excited." Well, when I look back I am grateful to God for my husband, our two daughters and the life we had as a family. When I look forward I am excited for the opportunities that lie ahead for my grandchildren and great-grandchildren.

BORN *December 4, 1931*

annie crocker

A favorite quote that I heard Steve Jobs and others use is, "Anyone can give up, it's the easiest thing to do. But to hold it together when everyone else would understand if you fell apart, that's true strength."

BORN *July 3, 1938*

francis austin

Growing up, I was blessed

with loving caring parents, teachers, professors, friends and mentors. Happy memories of the fun I had with classmates are remembrances that always go with me. We studied together, stayed in contact with each other and we have each other as a support group to this day.

My desire to pursue education came from my mama, the pursuit of entrepreneurship from my father. This has been made clearer to me as I have gotten older.

Mama instilled in me that a college education was a must-have, not an option. She graduated from Benedict College in South Carolina in 1929, the same year my parents were married. My father always encouraged my three sisters and me to have our own real estate, our own piece of land.

BORN May 2, 1937

mattie giles

I never could have made it—never would have made it—without my spiritual foundation.

I am truly grateful to be here. The youngest of 11 children, seven brothers and three sisters. I no longer have any siblings left but I have four incredible children who all graduated from military academies. My three sons graduated from West Point and my daughter graduated from the Naval Academy.

BORN *June 11, 1935*

june turner

I have so much gratitude for the profound impact that a non-biological "aunt" had on my life. My mother passed when I was 25 and this woman came into my life through marriage and remained steadfast for 44 years (until her death). She was my rock and my salvation, always understanding and compassionate. She kept me constantly uplifted by always telling me, "God is going to put a star in your crown."

BORN *February 6, 1930*

elaine neal

I was the youngest of 11 children. I loved to read and learn and always had a book or pencil with me. I was determined to get an education. I attended Princess Anne Academy, later to become Princess Anne College and now it is part of the University of Maryland system. My sisters did domestic work to help me go to and stay in college. While attending the academy I cleaned bathrooms, scrubbed floors, and did everything I could to earn money to stay in school.

BORN *December 9, 1917*

mary west

I am grateful for the lessons

I have learned. I am grateful for the level of intelligence and the ability to endure and fare above the challenges I have experienced as a black woman. I am grateful for my commitment to making a difference in other's lives.

Remembering African-American history is truly a gift to me as it enables me to understand from where I come: Harriet Tubman, Sojourner Truth, my mother and so many more.

Life is really about lessons. I am most proud of the fact that I have no fear in my life. I reflect on the challenges I've encountered, all of which I've risen above, being able to handle them to my benefit. I am so grateful, and gratitude can transform your life.

I am so pleased and proud to have lived 71 years and see the fruits of my labor, my children, grandchildren and community. Now I am so peaceful, a sense of fulfillment surrounds me that is really hard to express—a wonderful place to be at this point in time. I feel great and grateful. I am blessed. And even with that, every day, I know the best is still yet to come.

BORN *February 27, 1940*

doris

True friends are a special gift.

Good friends listen, offering help when needed in good and bad times. I have confidence in my friends. I have a friend who is godmother to my son and we have been friends for over 50 years. A true friend sticks by you like real family.

BORN *October 16, 1930*

catherine robinson

We moved to Prince George's County, Maryland in 1967. We had some challenges moving into a mostly white neighborhood. Yet it was one of the white neighbors who got my husband to run for elected office. We still live in that same house.

BORN *August 2, 1927*

fleeta ruffin

I only had one child. If I knew then what I know now, I probably would have had more children. Children really do make a house a home.

BORN *December 28, 1915*

mollie sherrod

The best thing I did for myself was to become educated. I was always fascinated with school and loved to read. I recall an old saying from when I was growing up, "Put something in your head so you can make it out of the shed." I guess I was determined to make it out of the shed.

Music is soothing and I love it. Every day I play the organ, piano or keyboard. I have a concert for myself.

BORN *March 12th*

evelyn husbands

If I knew then what I know now ...

I have been fortunate to have lived in Europe and the Far East for extended periods of time because of my husband's Air Force career. In each place we lived I was struck by the friendliness and curiosity of the people my family encountered. However, our every-day encounters and travels would have been more substantive and enriched had we been fluent in the spoken languages.

With the changed ethnic makeup of our own country and communities, I wish I had concentrated on learn-ing other languages and studying other cultures. This thought comes to mind often as I struggle to converse intelligently with some of our neighbors. Today, I am delighted to see our schoolchildren learning and speaking languages that were not even taught when I was in school.

BORN *October 27, 1930*

norma *hill*

If I knew then what I know now .... prior to choosing a career or starting a family, I would have traveled and lived in several foreign countries. Experiencing other cultures enhances our sensitivity and understanding of people.

BORN September 15, 1940

elizabeth "susie" proctor

If I knew then what I know now ... I would have gotten my college degree for my own personal satisfaction, traveled more extensively, and delayed getting married until I had accomplished my personal goals.

BORN February 11, 1938

jacqueline tolson

When I was 17, I begged my very strict parents,

to allow me to travel from a very small protected community to New York where I would work as a sleep-in housekeeper. My hometown pastor helped me find a church in the city. I certainly enjoyed my stay in New York because there I could do things that I was not allowed to do at home. Things such as dancing or buying and wearing fashionable clothes.

Yet when I returned five years later, I was happy to be back in that small community with my parents. And they were much happier to see me return than they were to see me leave.

BORN *December 16, 1916*

ertha hopkins

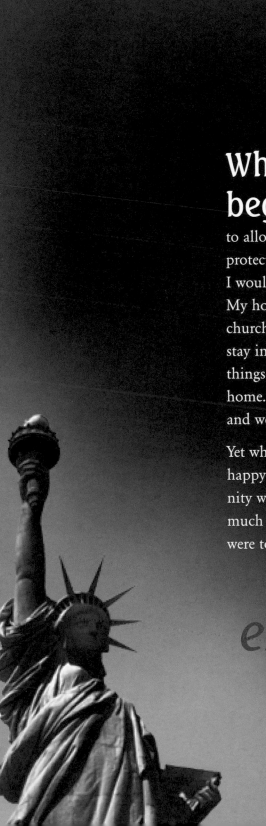

My most memorable experience

of all, is my weeklong trip to Paris, France. I had dreamed of going there since my days of French classes in high school. In 1994, my best friend from high school won the grand prize on "Wheel of Fortune" and asked me to accompany her on this fabulous journey.

We flew first-class, stayed at a grand hotel on the Champs Élysées, were treated to fine restaurants and visited all the famous sites. All in all, we felt like royalty! I am grateful for a wonderful friend and that my dream came true. I will never forget that trip of a lifetime.

My friend, now stricken with Alzheimer's, does not recall the trip at all.

BORN *August 19, 1922*

catherine
horn

Communication, planning and commitment to teamwork as a means of goal development and problem solving are the qualities I most respect and try to emulate as a leader. They are not complex, but it is often the simplest things that make the most difference.

BORN *November 21, 1926*

peola mccaskill

> Life is no "brief candle" for me.
> It is a sort of splendid torch which
> I have got hold of for the moment, and
> I want to make it burn as brightly as possible
> before handing it on to future generations.
> *– George Bernard Shaw –*

If I knew then what I know now, I would have taken my time to learn more about relationships and more about myself. I would have given myself the time to evolve and not tried to be too grown so early. And yet, I'm mindful that some of the mistakes I made allowed me to grow and be prepared for things to come. I view life as a growth experience and always seek to grow even during the hard times.

BORN *June 6, 1940*

I took care of my mother for 15 years. For 13 of those years she never spoke and was incapable of doing anything for herself. I also took care of my dad when he was sick. You see, I was an only child.

My son was diagnosed with cancer when he was 14 and he lived 17 years with cancer. When he was diagnosed, we were preparing for a trip to Europe and I was riding high. The whole family was going to Europe! I realized through that experience that material things were not important to me and I needed to give myself to a greater cause...off came my diamonds and all the trappings.

Early on in my life, I didn't believe I had a cross to bear and I took life for granted. After shouldering many painful crosses, if I knew then what I know now, I would have spent more time appreciating and spent more quality time with loved ones. I just would have put more into it than I did.

BORN *September 10, 1930*

frankie
newman

Every season my mother would make my sister and me seven dresses. Many of those dress patterns were copied from the designs in department stores. My mother knew how to look at an outfit and create a pattern to make a similar garment. She called that "making cloth." She also used that term in regard to life's journey. She would say, "Don't panic in a crisis. Just keep turning the problem around until you can make it fit or make it work for you."

BORN *December 2, 1926*

lauranita dugas

My beloved mother could give us, any of her 15 children, a good whipping. And then she would rub us down with Vaseline ... with love to soothe our wounds.

BORN *May 15, 1927*

daisy stith

I learned to can food from my mother, who learned to can from her mother.

BORN *February 25, 1926*

margaret gray

Sometimes I refer to myself as a Jack Daniels drinking, poker playing, Christian!

There are so many things I enjoy. Yet without a doubt, prayer is and has always been my number one priority.

I was married twice to two wonderful men who adored me. My first husband and I were married for 41 years. After he died my friends were constantly introducing me to eligible men. I remember telling one gentleman, as he was pursuing me, "I have a little house, a little money, a little car and I am a little satisfied."

I learned a long time ago to be thankful for what you have and don't worry about what you don't have. I never saw anyone I was jealous of. They have what they have, and so do I. They do what they do, and so do I.

BORN May 30, 1910

ollie miller phillips

I am grateful for the gift of life, good health, peace and happiness.

BORN *March 19, 1939*

beatrice leonard

There have been many material gifts in my life. But, I feel that the greatest gifts will always be the gifts of God's love, the love of family, and the love of true friends.

BORN *June 29, 1938*

naomi elliott

Don't let age keep you from trying something new. Age tries a new number every year.

BORN *November 11, 1929*

cynthia rollins

If I knew then what I know now

I would have been more attentive to the role of memory in our lives. While I have known that art, architecture, literature and monuments are what distinguish us as human and humane, I did not fully appreciate that the stuff we accumulate represents our basic need to mark our way of life. How else would we know who we are, remember whence we came, and prepare for descendants to go forward?

It is not just the memory that gets us from day to day and year to year. It is the remembrance of special relationships and challenging experiences that make us people.

Oral tradition is significant but in this fast-paced global society where discrimination and oppression against people of color have prevailed for centuries, we would be lost without books to clarify our history; photographs to portray how beautiful we are; diaries to capture our thoughts, emotions and experiences; artifacts to represent places we have been; keepsakes to reveal our creativity; and monuments to help us celebrate acts of courage.

If I knew then what I know now I would have been more discriminating about the stuff I saved, and it would have been labeled. Stories about people in our lives would have been shared with my grandchildren. And surely there should have been much less stuff accumulated for them to ponder and discard in the trash of our "civilization."

It would be wise to remind yourself that it is always timely to identify and record that which is truly precious so that our collective memory is enriched and preserved.

BORN August 14, 1920

joyce turner

If I knew then what I know now, I would have used my younger days more effectively, not married so early, pursued a career in counseling. Yet I must say, I prepared for retirement. I started watching my money early and began by saving dimes. Then I graduated to saving more wisely. Now, I don't want for anything at all. Glory to God!

BORN *January 11, 1938*

edna poney

My father died when I was very young and my mother and grandmother raised us. My brothers, sisters and I called them "the judge and the jury." All their decisions and verdicts were final, yet everything they did or said was surrounded in love and godliness. That was the foundation that allowed me to run a successful business for over fifty years.

BORN *June 28th*

gladys horne

I had good parents who led me in the right directions. They taught me that I had to work for what I wanted, and that is what I have done all of my grown life. It has paid off for me because I had a house built for my retirement years and have been living in it for the last 19 years.

BORN *October 16, 1928*

marie cooper

There were only two things

that I really ever wanted—to dance and to marry the man that I married. All my blessings are from those two things, including my children and grandchildren.

I have always danced and was blessed with the opportunity to study, create, perform and teach dance. African American classical dancing was my experience, my art and my vision— a true expression of *American* dance.

BORN *March 8, 1933*

eva anderson

I am grateful for my parents because from them I gained strength, a sense of reasoning and an appreciation for life. If I knew then what I know now, I would not change a thing!

BORN *January 10, 1929*

ertie barnes

If I knew then what I know now, I would not have made a commitment to marriage at such an early age. I would have completed some of my strong interests first, like pursuing and completing higher education. I did pursue evening courses, but not like I wish I had.

BORN *July 16, 1936*

mary budd

I have been in the same church for 37 years. I came to this church with my husband because I believe families should worship together. Now that's all I am going to say about husbands. They are dead now and I am not looking for a live one.

BORN *June 9, 1917*

louie dell clark

if i knew then
what i know now

... I would have kept written information about my family history. I now know it is important to know your ancestors' accomplishments.

My parents were very active in the community, my father was president of the civic association for as long as I can remember. My mother was the first black social worker in Memphis, Tennessee. All of us—all eight of their children—graduated college.

BORN July 26, 1922

lucy b. warr

I would have been proud of my heritage. I would have appreciated the culture, the character and color of my heritage. If I had known then of the struggles, the strength, the strides and achievements of my heritage I would have been proud of myself as a person. I would have told all of my friends to be yourself and strive to become the best of what you can be.

constance sturgis

If I knew then what I know now, I would
have devoted more quality time to my children during their
developmental years. It appears that one is always racing from
one phase to another without really understanding who these
little individuals are. As we spend so much time getting our
careers and lives together we devote less time with our children.
And before one realizes it those little people have grown up.

A lot of years have passed and I am still pondering some of the
actions I should have taken or some I should not have taken
to provide a greater influence on their lives. Although all my
children have grown to be superb adults, I can only imagine
what they could have been had I been a better parent.

BORN *June 30, 1935*

barbara

I have five incredible grandsons, but if you
think they are awesome you would have to
know their awesome parents. My children,
one son and five daughters, were wonderful
to raise, not perfect, but truly wonderful. I
respected them and I think they knew that.

If I knew then what I know now, I
would be a little different with the
children. I spent more time with the
girls than I did with my sons. I would
change that. I am very proud of my
children—but what if?

Together

WRITTEN BY ALBERTA LOUISE SEYMOUR A FEW SCORES AGO
(Photo of younger Seymour on left)

One day as I was strolling along the city street,

I saw a lady aged and gray and we two chanced to meet.

Then we two continued together on our way,

And I know we presented quite a picture upon the street that day.

There she was so aged that the years she could not hide,

And I bubbling over with youth still we strolled on side by side.

I guess in her memory she reflected she was once young without care

And I in my mind was thinking someday I may be like her.

So thus age and youth continued along the street that day

Until they happened to come to the parting of their way.

Both knew that age and youth could not synonymous be,

Yet they must travel hand in hand to the door of eternity.

BORN April 4, 1911

alberta louise seymour

about the author

Dorothy Bailey is a passionate woman of service and a woman of faith. She has founded several community organizations and remains involved with local, national and international efforts today. Ms. Bailey is active in her sorority, Alpha Kappa Alpha, Inc. and her church, Hunter Memorial African Methodist Episcopal Church. She chairs The LEARN Foundation, is president of the Prince George's Truth Branch of the Association for the Study of African Life and History (ASALH), and serves on the Board for the Kiamsha Youth Empowerment Organization.

She has been recognized by *Washingtonian Magazine* as one of the area's most powerful women. As an elected official, Bailey represented the citizens of Prince George's County (Maryland) on the County Council for eight years.

Ms. Bailey graduated from North Carolina Central University, where she was involved in the civil rights movement, and did postgraduate work at Pennsylvania State University and the University of Maryland. Bailey also received an Honorary Doctorate of Divinity from Riverside Baptist College and Seminary and serves on the board of directors for Maple Spring Baptist College and Seminary.

IN A DIFFERENT LIGHT is not her first undertaking as a writer. In 2005, she wrote and performed an uplifting spiritual play, "A Trilogy of Faith: The Victorious Stories of Leah, Rahab, and Virginia."

Bailey and her husband have two treasured children, three incredible grandchildren and a terrific grandniece. She lives in Temple Hills, Maryland.

dorothy f. bailey

The Wise Women Project.com

CIPRIANA THOMPSON Photographer

Cipriana has had a passion for photography for as long as she can remember. She loves the opportunity to challenge people to take another look or listen—to see from a new perspective that which perhaps they have seen and heard many times before. Cipriana's eye for portraiture and genuine fascination with people and their stories continue to push her forward in her pursuits. Along with years of experience, Cipriana completed professional training at the Washington School of Photography. Based out of the Washington, DC metropolitan area, she is a freelance photographer and owner of Soulfully Speaking Productions, specializing in both visual and written creative works.

TERRENCE NELSON Photographer

Terrence is a portrait photographer based in Prince George's County, Maryland. He is a full-time dad who loves to travel and meet new people. He is constantly working on different photo projects including a coffee table book showcasing his work over the last 10 years. The experience of photographing the women for this project has been moving and inspirational for him. He says, "If these women could achieve success and greatness in an era where all the chips were stacked against them—not just because they were black, but because they were black and female—then none of us has an excuse for failure today."

TIFFANY MORAND Licensed Skin Care Specialist and Make-up Artist

As a skin care professional, Tiffany strongly believes in the power of positive self-image and commits herself to enhancing that of her clientele through customized services to address each individual's concern. Tiffany was professionally trained at the Aveda Institute in Washington, D.C. Her knowledge and skills have been developed through 15 years of experience creating glamorous looks for theatre casts, bridal parties, and various models during photo shoots. At her clinic Dollface Skincare and Esthetics, located in Upper Marlboro, Maryland, Tiffany focuses on the importance of maintaining a consistent skin care regimen and educates clients on lifestyle habits that promote healthy, beautiful skin.

VALERIE WOODY Photographer

In 1990, after years of amateur picture taking, Valerie committed herself to the full-time pursuit of her artistic passion. With her remarkable daughter Jasmine as inspiration, she pursued every available educational opportunity and studied under the tutelage of a host of highly regarded professionals, including Sumner Rhodes, Monte Zucker, and Charles Lewis. Currently, she provides portrait, wedding, publicity and special event photography services to a multitude of satisfied clients throughout the mid-Atlantic region. Valerie believes that each subject has a unique and characteristic beauty. By artistically manipulating light and shadows, she strives to capture that beauty in the most memorable and extraordinary manner possible.

Thompson, Nelson and Morand worked as a team to photograph most of the women in the book. Woody is credited with photographing Robinson (p.72), Hopkins (p.76), Phillips (p.82) and Seymour (p.93).